Ugly Bugs & Apple Trees

Ugly Bugs & Apple Trees

12 ready-to-use assemblies for primary schools

Michael Catchpool
and Pat Lunt

kevin
mayhew

First published in 2002 by
KEVIN MAYHEW LTD
Buxhall, Stowmarket, Suffolk IP14 3BW
Email: info@kevinmayhewltd.com

9 8 7 6 5 4 3 2 1

ISBN 1 84003 899 3
Catalogue No 1500504

Cover design by Angela Selfe
Edited by Elisabeth Bates
Typesetting by Louise Selfe

Printed and bound in Great Britain

Contents

About the authors

Michael Catchpool is a headteacher and, as a result, has done the odd assembly (very odd, some people say).

Pat Lunt teaches in a Junior school and knows a thing or two about assemblies as well (and not just the way it is spelt . . . and that strictly speaking it should be called 'collective worship'). He has responsibility for RE and PSHME in his school.

They have collaborated on a number of projects and are the authors of the bestselling *Kings and Monkeys* as well as *Say It, Act It!*, Books 1 and 2 (a useful drama resource for schools) and *The Log in My Eye*, a book of double-act sketches.

Introduction

Here is another collection of stories from the authors of *Kings and Monkeys*. Within these tales you will find kindly kings and foolish farmers, bickering brothers and wayward waiters and lots more besides.

As with the stories in *Kings and Monkeys*, they are intended to be used in two main ways.

First, they are an original and very useful resource for assemblies or collective worship. Each story is accompanied by a concluding piece, which explores the theme of the story and provides 'food for thought', for those moments of reflection. The theme is explored in general terms and, in addition, with a Christian emphasis, so that those leading the session may choose the most appropriate for their situation.

Second, the stories are equally useful as a valuable resource for PSHME (Personal, Social, Health and Moral Education). Each story can be used as a starting point to help explore a particular issue. In addition, there is a selection of questions at the end of each story to aid or prompt discussion.

However you choose to use this book, our hope is that it is accessible, fun and a stress-free resource for the busy teacher.

The king's new gift

Story It was King Frederick's birthday. And even though he was king, just like most people on their birthday, King Frederick was excited.

'I wonder what presents I shall get?' said King Frederick to himself. 'I hope they are better than last year's.'

'Last year I got a golden eggcup from the Lord Chamberlain . . . and I don't even like boiled eggs. I got a special hand-knitted cosy for my crown to keep it warm and some special writing paper with my picture on it, which I had to use to write all my thank-you letters on. No, I just hope there's something a little bit more interesting.'

After a royal breakfast, at which all the servants had wished him a happy birthday and the royal cook had made a special birthday pancake with *'Happy birthday Your Majesty'* on it in maple syrup, the trumpeters blew a fanfare and King Frederick's presents were brought in.

The king unwrapped them one by one. He was very excited.

Well, he was until he unwrapped the pair of socks knitted in royal blue with a crown motif on the side . . . and he wasn't quite so excited when he unwrapped the mug with *'King Frederick's Coffee Mug'* written on the side. Nor was he very excited when he opened the present which turned out to be a hot water bottle with its own carry case embroidered with his own royal coat of arms.

Eventually, King Frederick had opened all his presents except one. There was just one left and it lay on the table. King Frederick picked it up. 'I wonder what it is,' he thought to himself. Curious, King Frederick unwrapped the present. He held it up and turned to his servant: 'It's magnificent,' said the king, still holding it up high in the air. 'It's truly magnificent.' And then he added, 'Um, what is it?'

'It is a flute, Your Majesty,' said the servant, 'a flute.'

'I see,' said King Frederick. 'How exciting, a flute. I have never had one of those before. This is wonderful! I know what I shall do – I shall place it on a special royal cushion and I shall look at it every day. That's exactly what I shall do. I would hate to get it dirty.'

'But just a moment, Your Majesty,' said one servant, 'aren't you going to pick it up and play it?'

'I beg your pardon?' said the king.

'Aren't you going to play it? That's what you're supposed to do with a flute.'

'Oh no,' said the king, 'I've never played a flute before, I don't know what to do. I've no idea, it all sounds a bit scary. No, I don't think I'll do that. I shall just leave it on its royal cushion where it can't get dirty.'

'But, Your Majesty,' continued the servant, 'it would be such a shame, for you can play such wonderful music on it.'

'I see,' said King Frederick, 'and how do I do that?'

'Well,' explained the servant, 'you have to blow into it.'

'Oh no,' said the king. 'No, no, no, I'm not doing that, I've never done that before. I might get it all wrong and then people would laugh at me. No, I'm definitely not going to do that. What I will do is leave it on its royal cushion so I can look at it. In that way I can be sure it will never get dirty and no one will laugh at me.'

But the servant had more to say. 'But Your Majesty, that flute will let you play beautiful music. Now you might not be able to manage it straight away, but if you practise you would be able to do it, I'm sure.'

'Practise, whatever do you mean?' said King Frederick, most surprised.

'Well, practise, you know, trying to play your flute every day, practising scales and simple tunes, and, as you get better, longer and more difficult pieces. If you practised every day, I'm sure you could do it.'

'Oh no, no, no,' said King Frederick, shaking his head, 'I certainly don't like the sound of that; *practise every day*, sounds like an awful lot of hard work to me. No, my mind is made up – I will leave my flute on its royal cushion; that way I know it won't get dirty, I won't have to try blowing into it, people won't laugh if I get it wrong and I won't have to do lots of practising which sounds like far too much hard work. My new flute will stay on its royal cushion.'

And indeed it did. And I'm told that if you go to the palace today, King Frederick's flute still lies untouched and unplayed on its royal cushion.

General theme   We often face new things in life – new opportunities, new challenges. I wonder how we respond to them? King Frederick responded to his new flute in a very odd way. Rather than enjoying it and learning to play it, he chose to keep it on a cushion, untouched. He got very anxious – he didn't want to get things wrong, he didn't want to have to practise hard – it all seemed far too much. Are we like that? Are we scared to try new challenges in case we get things wrong? Are we not prepared to put in the hard work it might need to succeed? It would be a shame if we were. King Frederick really missed out, his present was wasted. May we be the sort of people who do not waste the new opportunities we face each day but instead persevere with them, even though they may be difficult to begin with.

Christian theme

We can face new challenges, new opportunities each day. Just like King Frederick, we can sometimes become daunted by them or worried. But what a shame if we missed the chance because we were worried that we might get something wrong or felt we couldn't put in the effort needed.

Whilst facing new challenges can be daunting, the Bible says that we do not have to face them alone – Jesus says, 'I am with you even unto the end of the age.' (Matthew 28:20)

PSHME ideas

This story can be used to discuss:

- Opportunities
- New beginnings
- Facing challenges
- Perseverance

- How do you feel when you are faced with something new?
- Have you been nervous of trying something new but had a go anyway? How did you feel afterwards?
- What things have you had to practise so that you could improve?
- Some people who feel nervous about doing something try to imagine a calm scene. What tricks do you have to help you when you are nervous?

Frank and Ernest

Story There was once a restaurant called *The Blue Candle*. No one really knew why it was called *The Blue Candle*, not even the owner, Mr Higgins. He named it but he couldn't remember why. Working in *The Blue Candle* were two waiters called Frank and Ernest. Frank worked on Mondays, Wednesdays and Fridays. Ernest worked on Tuesdays, Thursdays and Saturdays. Frank and Ernest were good waiters . . . they were fast waiters – very fast indeed.

Whenever Frank worked he would say to himself, 'I am by far the best waiter in this restaurant . . . the best and the fastest. I will always be first and no one's ever going to get in my way.'

And when it was Ernest's turn to work, he would stand in the restaurant and say to himself, 'I am by far the best waiter in this restaurant . . . the best and the fastest. I will always be first and no one's ever going to get in my way.'

On Monday, Frank set to work in *The Blue Candle*. He rushed down the narrow corridor that led from the kitchens to the tables where the customers were sitting. He was so fast that the customers hardly had time to choose from the menu before he was off, straight back down the narrow corridor to the kitchens and back again with the order.

Frank was so fast that if you ordered soup it was still so piping hot from the pan it would burn your mouth, it had no time to cool down at all.

And almost before the customers had a chance to finish their starter, he whipped away their plates and rushed off down the narrow corridor to the kitchens and back again with their main course.

And just as the customers were putting their last chip, or piece of potato or carrot into their mouths, Frank would whip away their plates, dash down the narrow corridor to the kitchen and return with their dessert – oh yes, Frank was a very fast waiter.

On Tuesday, it was Ernest's turn to work in *The Blue Candle*. Ernest was just as fast as Frank. He rushed down the narrow corridor that led from the kitchens, took the customers' orders and was off again like a shot. Ernest was so fast that if you ordered prawn cocktail, the prawns were almost still wriggling on the plate when you got it. And almost before the customers had a chance to even finish their starter, Ernest would clear away their plates and dash down the narrow corridor that led to the kitchen and return with their main courses and then their dessert. And before they knew it, the customers were paying the bill almost before they'd even sat down, it was all over so fast.

'I am the very best waiter and the fastest,' Ernest said to himself, 'I shall always be first and no one's going to get in my way.'

And so the two waiters went on their merry and very fast way, both thinking to themselves that they were the best and the fastest and that no one was going to get in their way.

And things would have carried on that way, if Mr Higgins hadn't one day agreed to host a special meal at his restaurant for the Mayor, his wife, and all the local dignitaries.

Mr Higgins said to himself, 'With all these special guests, I will need all hands on deck.' And though it was a Saturday, he rang both Frank and Ernest and asked them if they could both work.

Frank and Ernest stood waiting near the kitchens whilst the Mayor, his wife, and all the local dignitaries made their way, very grandly, into *The Blue Candle*.

The Mayor sat down, and so did his wife and so did all the dignitaries and Mr Higgins proudly handed them each a menu.

Meanwhile, Frank and Ernest stood waiting.

Frank looked at Ernest and he thought to himself, 'Who on earth does he think he is? I am the best waiter, I am the fastest, I shall be first because I am very important and nothing's going to get in the way. I can see it all now. I shall serve the Mayor and he will think I am magnificent and leave me an enormous tip.'

And all the time that Frank was looking at Ernest, Ernest was looking at Frank. 'Who on earth does that Frank think he is? I am the best waiter, I am the fastest. I shall be the first because I am very important and nothing's going to get in the way. Oh yes, I can see it all. I shall serve the Mayor and his wife and they will think I am wonderful and they will leave me an enormous tip.'

Both Frank and Ernest stood by the doors to the kitchen waiting. Through the glass door at the end of the narrow corridor they could see the Mayor and his wife and all the local dignitaries looking through the menu. They could see Mr Higgins standing next to them. Suddenly, Mr Higgins held up his hand. That was the signal, they were ready to place their orders.

'I want to be first,' thought Frank, 'I want to be first!' and off he shot down the narrow corridor.

'I will be first, I deserve to be first!' thought Ernest and off he sped down the narrow corridor at exactly the same time as Frank.

But oh dear, it certainly was a narrow corridor, a corridor that was so narrow there was just not room for two people to go down it together – and as Frank and Ernest tried, they got wedged in, their shoulders jammed against each other and squashed against the wall.

'Get out of the way!' Frank shouted at Ernest. 'Get out of the way! I am more important than you, I'm a much better waiter than you. I should be first, now move!'

But Ernest couldn't; instead he shouted at Frank. 'You get out of my way, I'm much more important than you! I'm a better waiter so I must go first, now move!'

But Frank couldn't move either. They were squashed in, side by side in the narrow corridor as tight as a cork in a bottle.

Meanwhile, the Mayor and his wife and all the local dignitaries sat waiting for someone to take their order. They waited and they waited and when a waiter still didn't arrive, they stood up in a grand huff and said to a rather forlorn Mr Higgins, 'This is a disgrace, there is no one in this restaurant to take our orders; what useless waiters you have, we are off!' And indeed they were – out they went, leaving Mr Higgins alone in *The Blue Candle*.

Mr Higgins stormed off to find out what had happened to Frank and Ernest and he found them still wedged in side by side in the narrow corridor. 'What on earth are you doing here?' he shouted. 'You have ruined the whole evening. My most important guests have left because no one came to take their order and serve them. What were you doing?'

'Well, I was trying to be first,' Frank mumbled, a little embarrassed.

'And I was trying to be first, too,' Ernest said.

'Well, you *can* be first, both of you,' said Mr Higgins. 'You can be the first two waiters I sack! Now both of you out, I don't ever want you in my restaurant again!'

And with a huge shove from behind, Mr Higgins got Frank and Ernest unstuck and out of the door of *The Blue Candle*. And they have not been back since.

General theme   Frank and Ernest got themselves into all sorts of bother. How different it might have been if Frank had been prepared to say, 'After you, Ernest.' Or if Ernest had said to Frank, 'You go first.' But to do that, they needed to stop thinking about themselves, how important they felt they were and think about each other. I wonder if we are like that, and spend so much time thinking about ourselves that we do not seem to care about other people. Are we so concerned about being first, getting things for ourselves, that we miss what others need? We can begin to show our respect for others by even the simplest of actions; by holding a door open for someone, by letting someone past, by a 'please' or a 'thank-you'. And whilst these actions may seem simple, they actually show something very important: that you value and respect others enough to put them first for a change . . . now that is a challenge!

Christian theme

Do we always want to be first? Do we think we are so much more important than everybody else? It's what Frank and Ernest thought and it caused real problems. Wouldn't it have made a difference if they had stopped to think about how they would have liked to be treated? Would they have behaved differently? I'm sure they would.

Putting others first is sometimes a real challenge; in the Bible, Jesus spent so much of his time not worrying about himself but showing care and respect for others, valuing them so that they could feel important; and he encouraged his followers to do the same. He said that to be the greatest, we need to be ready to help and serve others. What a difference if we could do that for each other. Even the simplest of gestures, like holding a door open, or a 'please' or 'thank-you', can begin to show the value and respect we can have for others. Can we respond to the challenge of putting others first?

PSHME ideas

This story can be used to discuss:

- Courtesy
- Valuing others
- Competition

- How do you feel when you manage to be first?
- How important is it for you to be first?
- How does it make you feel when someone does something kind for you?
- What do you think 'putting others first' means?

The king who had no time to be king

There was once a king who lived in a fine castle with towers and turrets that reached up to the sky. The king had everything he could wish for. He had a fine golden carriage, pulled by a troop of magnificent white horses, and servants who ran this way and that for him – even before he'd asked for anything. He had a wonderful chef, who prepared the most sumptuous meals . . . and a special chef whose job it was just to make chocolate eclairs, with fresh cream – because there was nothing the king liked more than chocolate eclairs with fresh cream. He had soldiers who marched up and down and saluted him, he had musicians to play delightful tunes to cheer him up if he felt sad, or to help him sleep if he felt fretful. He had a magnificent four-poster bed and so did his dog. He had gardeners who tended his palatial grounds, mowing the lawns, weeding the borders and clipping the yew hedges into fantastic shapes – including one that looked just like him.

He even had a golden eggcup with a golden egg-spoon, and as for his toilet seat . . . well you wouldn't believe it.

But there was one thing the king did not have – and that was a queen.

One day the king got up and announced to his servants, who stood ready with his freshly ironed royal clothes, 'It is about time I got married. Send out a royal declaration that I, the King, intend to get married in two months' time.'

'But, Your Majesty,' said the servants, 'it's not as easy as that.'

'Whatever do you mean?' said the king.

'Well, before you get married, you must find someone whom you love and who loves you.'

'I see,' said the king. 'Well, call all the local princesses to the castle and I shall see if there is anyone amongst them whom I could marry.'

'Right away, Your Majesty,' said the servants, and off they went and set about the task. They rode out from the castle with the king's royal proclamation that he intended to get married.

It was not long before a queue of princesses turned up at the castle gates.

The king greeted them all; and though he spoke with them and even danced with them all at a royal banquet, there was none there that he felt he could marry.

Until suddenly, there was a knock on the castle door. And in came one more princess.

'I'm sorry I'm late,' she said, 'I'm afraid I had to help my father with the milking'. (She wasn't a very rich princess.)

The king danced with her and spent the rest of the evening talking to her. She told him of her life at home, collecting the eggs from the hens (they couldn't afford servants to do that) and helping with the ploughing (they couldn't afford servants to do that either . . . she really was a very poor princess).

But as she talked, the king soon realised that . . . that he was falling in love.

The next day the king spent all the time he had with the poor princess and it seemed that she too was falling in love.

'At last,' thought the king, 'I shall have a queen,' and he was very pleased, very pleased indeed.

It wasn't long before preparations were being made for the royal wedding. The soldiers practised their marching and drill, as they were to lead the royal wedding procession. The princess watched from the balcony as the soldiers marched by in their red uniforms; she remarked to the king how smart the soldiers looked and how clever they were to remember all the different manoeuvres.

'I see,' said the King, 'I see.' And he hurried off to the royal tailor. 'I want you to make me a red uniform just like the soldiers wear.'

'At once, Your Majesty,' the tailor replied and off he went. He soon returned with a uniform fit for a king (which was lucky really, since that was who it was for). And indeed, it did fit, very well. The king put it on and at once he asked the captain of the guards to teach him some of the manoeuvres. The king practised long and hard. When the princess asked if he would be joining her for dinner, he replied that he was too busy and off he went to practise some more.

The next day, the royal trumpeters were out practising the royal fanfare they were going to play at the wedding. It sounded magnificent.

'Aren't those trumpeters clever,' remarked the princess.

'I see,' said the king, 'I see.' And he rushed to the chief trumpeter and said, 'You must find me a trumpet right away and then teach me to play.'

'At once, Your majesty,' said the chief trumpeter, and it was not long before he returned with a trumpet fit for . . . well, a king. Which was just as well, for that is who it was for.

The chief trumpeter showed the king how to play and gave him lots of scales and tunes to practise.

'Won't you come for a walk in the garden?' asked the princess.

'No, no,' said the king, 'I am much too busy.'

The next day, the princess stood on the balcony and laughed and clapped with delight as she watched the jugglers practise their performance for the royal wedding celebrations.

'Aren't they wonderful?' she enthused, 'How clever they are.'

'I see, I see,' muttered the king, and he hurried off and straight-away sought out one of the jugglers – the one who could juggle seven clubs whilst balancing a teacup on his head.

'Will you teach me to juggle?' asked the king.

'Why of course, Your Majesty,' said the juggler. (Well, what else could he say to the king?)

'Won't you come for a ride into the village so we could choose some flowers for the wedding?' asked the princess.

'I'm afraid not,' said the king, 'I am far too busy.'

Every morning the king would practise his trumpet, playing scales and tunes. In the afternoon, he would practise his military manoeuvres (resplendent in his uniform). And in the evening he would practise his juggling, with clubs and juggling balls – though the teacups proved rather tricky.

And though the princess often asked if she could spend the day with him, he was always far too busy.

One evening, as the king sat down to a late supper after a busy day of trumpet playing and marching and juggling, he found a note on his dinner plate – just next to his slice of chicken pie. It simply read:

Your Majesty,

I have decided to leave, for I fell in love with a wonderful king, but now that king seems to have disappeared. Instead there is just one more soldier, one more trumpeter, and one more juggler. The king has gone, and if the king has gone, I may as well go too.

Signed, The Princess.

And indeed she did!

General theme   What a pity for the king. He had so much, but in the end he lost it all. The princess loved him and was ready to be his wife, but he thought he needed to change – to be able to juggle or play the trumpet or march, to be like someone else. He just couldn't believe that the princess was interested in him for who he was.

Sometimes we can be so concerned about trying to be like other people – people we see on television or in magazines or in films – that we end up thinking that we are not any good ourselves; that the only way we can be of worth is if we become like somebody else. But it is very important to realise our own value, our own self-worth, because we are all special and important.

And just as we can value ourselves and realise how important and special we are, we can help others feel good about themselves by the way we treat them too.

Christian theme

How strange, a king who had everything but lost it all because he just couldn't believe he was good enough for the princess. He thought she would like him so much better if he could juggle or play the trumpet or march expertly, but it just wasn't true. She loved him for who he was. Sometimes we find it hard to really value ourselves. The Bible tells us that God thinks everyone of us is very special indeed. In fact, it says that God knows even the number of hairs on our head, that's how important we are to him. If God, who created the whole world, thinks we are important, then we really must be. And as we accept that we are valued and special, we can help others realise just how important they are by the way we treat them as well.

PSHME ideas

This story can be used to discuss:

- Self-esteem
- Relationships
- Making an impression
- Talents

- What things are you really good at?
- What things do you wish you were really good at?
- Can you think of someone you wish you were like? Why do you think you want to be like them?
- Lots of people find it much easier to talk about the things they can't do, rather than the things they can, why do you think that is?
- What have you done that you are most proud of?

The new king

Story   The villagers of Dunstonville were very excited. They had been
told a new king was to take up the throne.

'I wonder what he will be like?' asked the blacksmith's wife as
she hung out the washing.

'I know just what he'll be like,' her husband replied. 'He will
be strong and brave – a powerful king. And so I will make him a
special present – a magnificent sword, keen-edged, with a huge
handle. He will be able to grip his sword with both hands and
smite his enemies. He'll smite them to the left and he'll smite
them to the right, because that's what a real king does!'

And the blacksmith set to work at his forge and anvil hammering
out the red hot metal to make a sword fit for a king.

In his workshop, the jeweller turned to his wife and said, 'Have
you heard the news? A new king is on his way.'

'I know,' said his wife, 'it's very exciting. I do wonder what he'll
be like.'

'Oh, I know exactly what he'll be like. He'll be noble and proud,
you mark my words,' replied the jeweller. 'That is why I am going
to make him a special present – a magnificent crown. I will make it
from finely hammered gold, and it will be covered with precious
stones – red and green and blue. He will be able to wear it in
processions so that everyone can see just how noble he is, for
that is what a real king does.' And so the jeweller gathered up his
tools and set to work at once.

Meanwhile, the cobbler sat in his shop with his wife. 'I can't
wait,' she said, 'for the arrival of this new king; everybody's talking
about it.'

'I know, I know,' said the cobbler, 'it is very exciting.'

'But I wonder what he'll be like?' his wife continued.

'Oh, I know exactly what he'll be like. He'll be sophisticated,
used to the luxuries of life. He won't have to set foot on the wet
muddy streets, like you or me. He will walk on fine, plush carpets,
because that is what a king does. And that is why I am going to make
him a pair of velvet slippers with gold thread and embroidered

with a royal coat of arms.' And the cobbler set to work searching out his finest, softest velvet.

Down at the stables the farmer was talking to the stable-hand. 'It's exciting news about this new king,' said the farmer.

'Yes it is, I wonder what he'll be like.'

'I know exactly what he'll be like; he'll be a skilled horseman, riding up high on his saddle, away from the common people. He'll set himself apart, let people know just how important he is; he'll let them know his true position, for that is what a real king does. And so I am going to give him a special present, a fine white stallion, groomed and presented in the finest royal livery.'

The blacksmith, the jeweller, the cobbler and the farmer all worked hard at preparing their gifts, until the day the new king was due to arrive.

There was great excitement in the village and crowds came to meet the new king. Lining the streets, they cheered and called as he approached.

The blacksmith, the jeweller, the cobbler and the farmer stood among the excited crowd, eager to catch their first glimpse of the new king.

Suddenly, the farmer called out in utter surprise. 'Hang on, there must be some sort of mistake. That can't be the king. The king should be riding up high, proud in his saddle, looking majestic as he looks down on his subjects from his horse. But look at him! I can't believe it, he's sat riding a donkey! What kind of king does that? That's not the sort of king I was expecting and it's not the king I want – I want a proud king! Well, there's no way he's going to have my present!' And so the farmer turned away sadly and disappeared into the crowd.

The cobbler watched as the crowd jostled and pushed, trying to get a better view of the new king.

'That can't be right,' said the cobbler as he stood on tip-toe and peered over the people in front. 'Look at him. A king shouldn't be walking along the dirty, muddy roads like that, he should have a red carpet spread out before him to walk on. But him, he's now walking down there, of all places, and we all know the sort of people who live down there. A king should be sophisticated, not behaving like that. No, no, that's not the sort of king I was expecting and it's not the king I want. There's no way he's having my present.' And the cobbler turned away in disgust and disappeared into the crowd.

More and more people gathered, cheering loudly as the king came past. But the jeweller did not join in with the cheers.

As he looked, his face fell. 'This is supposed to be the king, but where are his magnificent robes, his velvet cloak? His clothes are far too plain and simple. Why, he almost looks just like one of the crowd. I'll not waste my present on him. This is not the king I was expecting and it's not the king I want!' And so saying, he turned away and disappeared into the crowd.

The blacksmith had happily joined the eager crowd who lined the streets and as he craned his neck to see the king his face suddenly fell in disappointment. 'Look, just look at him. Doesn't he know who those people are. Doesn't he know what they're like? He shouldn't be talking to them, they're the last people a king should be seen with. Just look, he almost seems to be going out of his way to talk to them. And look now, he is even shaking their hand! Those are the sort of people he should be getting rid of, driving them out of the kingdom. And yet he seems to be welcoming them. This just won't do, it won't do at all! Well, there's no way that he will be having my present. He is not the king I was expecting and he's not the king I want!' And the blacksmith turned and disappeared into the crowd.

And so, from that day on, the blacksmith and the jeweller, the cobbler and the farmer, never did get to meet the new king. They refused to have anything to do with him because, as they said, he was not the king they had expected and was not the king they wanted.

General theme

Some people think a leader needs to be big and strong, tall and powerful, just like some of the people in Dunstonville who wanted and expected a certain type of king. But some of the best-known leaders the world has seen have been quite different. Gandhi led a whole nation to independence, not by fighting with a mighty two-edged sword but by his quiet determination, his peaceful persistence. Nelson Mandela spent many years in prison before becoming the leader of South Africa. He led the country from its old and cruel regime of apartheid, not by riding a war horse, but by being ready to share what he felt was important with thousands of others through meeting with them and speaking to them.

Some of the most well-known leaders might not have immediately met people's expected ideas of what a leader should be like, but these leaders have become some of the greatest.

Christian theme

I wonder what you expect a great leader to be like – strong and powerful, rich and noble? That's certainly what some of the people in Dunstonville expected. But sometimes the greatest leaders can be very different.

I wonder how people felt when they first met Jesus. The Bible explains how he was not born in a royal palace, but in a stable. He was not rich; in fact, it says that whilst even foxes have holes for a home and birds have nests, Jesus had nowhere he could call a home (Luke 9:58). But the Bible also explains how Jesus is a king, and although a mighty king, someone who is prepared to talk to all sorts of people, to share and even to serve.

Do we only admire those who we think look important? Or can we see how powerful attributes such as humility, compassion, caring and patience can be?

PSHME ideas

This story can be used to discuss:

* Perceptions
* Expectations
* Stereotypes
* Power

* Which people do you think are the most powerful? Why?
* List three things you would expect a king to be like.
* Would it be better for a kingdom if the king was 2m tall or 1.6m?
* Can you think of a time when you decided not to speak to certain people because of what others thought about them?
* Have you ever spoken to someone or tried to be friends with someone, even when you knew your other friends didn't really like them?
* If you had to get someone to look after £10 for you, which of these three people would you ask: Dr Samuel Green, Revd Alistair Simons, or WPC Wendy Harris? Why?
* Can someone who is humble be a powerful person?

A good neighbour

Story There was once a man named Tom who moved from the city into the countryside. He had found a charming house in which to live and he was pleased to find that from his window he was able to see another house: not too close, but close enough for him to feel that he had a neighbour. Tom looked across at his neighbour's house and at its garden. The garden sloped down below the level of the wall and so it was impossible for Tom to see much of his neighbour's garden. But the tiny bit he could see looked delightful – a few small flowerbeds full of bright flowers and a trim, green, sloping lawn. Tom wondered if the rest of the garden, which was hidden behind the wall, was as well kept. He wondered too about the person who might live in such a house and have such a garden. It was not long before he found out.

One morning, as Tom looked from his window, he saw a kindly face appear slowly above the top of the wall at the end of his garden. And then a hand raised in a wave. Without a thought Tom waved back and smiled. The stranger at the wall beckoned him to come over. So Tom hurried downstairs and out into his garden. He ran the short distance across his lawn to the wall and gazed up at the friendly face.

'Hello,' smiled the man leaning over the wall. 'I'm Sheamus, your neighbour.'

'Hello, I'm Tom,' replied Tom.

'Pleased to meet you, Tom. I just thought I'd pop over to see how you were getting on. Settled in well?'

'Oh yes, quite well, thank you,' Tom replied.

'Good, good,' continued Sheamus. 'Well, I don't want to take up too much of your time. I'm sure you've still got plenty to do but I just brought you one or two things . . .'

He briefly disappeared below the top of the wall and then reappeared and stretched out his hand, holding a jar. 'Just a pot of home-made damson jam,' he said cheerily. 'I don't want to presume,' he went on, almost apologising, 'but if you ever want a chat . . . ,' (and he produced a small yellow flag), 'just wave the flag and I'll be able to come on over and meet you at this very spot.'

'That's very kind,' said Tom, taking the jam and the flag. 'Very kind indeed. I will certainly do that. And thank you very much for the jam.'

'Not at all, not at all,' smiled Sheamus. 'Anyway, best get back. You too, I daresay.'

And with the pleasantries over they each went back to their own home, with Tom holding on tight to the jar of damson jam and looking a little confused as he looked down at the yellow flag.

Tom, however, had no need of the yellow flag the next day, because Sheamus' cheery face appeared over the top of the wall that morning. 'Good morning Tom,' he called brightly.

Tom happily put down the work he was doing and made his way out of the house and across his short lawn to the wall and soon he and Sheamus were having a pleasant chat about this and that, and generally putting the world to rights.

And for the next few days this is exactly how things went on. Sheamus would appear at the wall and Tom would hurry over and they would chat about all sorts of things; Sheamus even brought with him another jar of damson jam for Tom.

One morning, Tom was busy weeding in his garden when he remembered the yellow flag that Sheamus had given him.

'I wonder what Sheamus must think of me,' he thought to himself. 'He's given me this flag and I've never used it; it always seems to be Sheamus who makes the effort to start our little chats. I hope he doesn't think I'm not interested. He's been so generous, making me feel so welcome and he's given me those lovely jars of damson jam. I will make the effort to call him over,' Tom thought. And he went inside, collected the yellow flag, went upstairs to the window and began waving it.

It wasn't long before he was greeted by the sight of Sheamus waving back from his window.

'Great, he's on his way,' Tom thought and he hurried over to the wall to wait. Tom waited and waited. Sheamus seemed to be taking a very long time.

'Perhaps he had something to finish off,' thought Tom. Anyway, he didn't mind too much. It was a nice day and he was looking forward to seeing Sheamus because he enjoyed their little chats. And sure enough, eventually Sheamus appeared, a little out of breath, but with a smile and ready to chat.

Over the next few days, Tom got quite used to waving the yellow flag from his window, and waiting for Sheamus to come to the wall for a chat.

And that was the problem. Tom felt he was having to do an awful lot of waiting. He would wave his flag and rush to the wall but it seemed to take ages for Sheamus to appear.

'Perhaps he was in no real hurry,' Tom thought to himself, and the more he thought about it, the angrier he became. 'He obviously thinks he has better things to do than rush over to see me. It's just not fair; whenever it's him who pops up over the wall wanting a chat, I rush straight over, but if I wave the flag he always keeps me waiting. I think he's just being rude. I'm not sure why I should bother really, if he can't be bothered for me.'

The final straw for Tom came when he desperately needed Sheamus' help. It had been raining all night, so much in fact that water had poured through Tom's roof and he needed a broom to sweep it out. He waved his flag to Sheamus whom he could just see at the window of his house. Sheamus waved back, so Tom set out for the wall. He drew his coat around his face against the wind which was blowing hard, and pulled his hat down over his forehead against the rain.

Tom reached the wall and waited for Sheamus. And waited. And waited. The longer he waited the colder and angrier he got. At last, after he felt he could wait no longer, he stamped angrily back to his own house muttering to himself.

He vowed he would have nothing more to do with Sheamus. After all, who needs a friend who can't be bothered to help when you need them?

And so from that day on, Tom put the flag away under his bed and left it there. And whenever Sheamus appeared over the top of the wall, waving and keen for a chat, Tom would turn his back and ignore him.

A few weeks later, as he glanced out of his window at the tiny patch of sloping garden that he could see by Sheamus' house, Tom saw a cart being loaded with possessions; and eventually, carrying one last armful, Sheamus came and sat on the cart and drove off into the distance, leaving the house empty and bleak.

'And good riddance to you too!' thought Tom.

A few days later, Tom decided he would satisfy his curiosity about what the rest of Sheamus' sloping garden looked like; he had still only managed to see the small patch up by the house. So Tom made his way to the wall where he had shared so many fine chats with Sheamus and began to climb it very carefully. The drystone wall was thick and strong but it was still a tricky climb as Tom was not very comfortable with heights. But he persevered and he was soon near the top. He pulled himself up and peered over the wall. What he saw made his face fall and his heart sink.

Below him, on the other side of the wall, was not a neat and pretty garden but a steep and treacherous gorge cut by a fast-flowing stream. And from the edge of the neat and tidy part of Sheamus' garden, steep stone steps plunged into that gorge. And at the foot of the steps, almost lost in the shadows, a small bridge, recently repaired, crossed the stream. On Tom's side of the gorge, by the bridge, steep uneven steps made the climb back up the gorge to a point just below the wall. And there rested a ladder on which Sheamus must have stood to have his conversations with Tom.

As he looked at the steep stone steps, Tom saw all too clearly why he had had to wait by the wall for Sheamus to come. And as he looked at the bridge so newly repaired, he realised why Sheamus had not come to the wall on the day of the storm.

Tom climbed slowly back down, turned to his house and walked back. His heart was heavy with thoughts of his good friend who had now gone away and his impatience with Sheamus. 'How could I have behaved like that?' he thought.

As he closed the door behind him, he just couldn't think of an answer.

General theme

It's very easy to judge people, to say they're wrong; to say they don't measure up to our expectations, particularly if we don't have the full picture. Tom was very quick to judge Sheamus, his neighbour – to accuse him of being lazy, of not being bothered. But little did he know that it was Sheamus who was making all the effort just to say 'hello'. Are we the sort of people who judge others when we don't know the full story? Or do we bother to take the time to find out just what efforts some people are making?

Christian theme

I wonder if we have ever been like Tom? Quick to judge . . . quick to accuse others – to say that they are at fault. What a pity Tom hadn't taken the time to see the full picture and realise just what efforts Sheamus was making. If anyone was at fault, then surely it was Tom. The Bible says that we shouldn't be quick to judge others, and also warns that sometimes, rather than notice small faults in others, we need to be ready to be aware that there may be some very big faults that we have and some very big changes that we need to make. (Matthew 7:1-5)

PSHME ideas   This story can be used to discuss:

- Judging others
- Perceptions
- Commitment
- Friendship
- Relationships

- What makes a good friend?
- What makes a friendship work and last?
- If you agreed to meet your friend at the shops at 9am and they turned up over half an hour late, how would you feel? What would you say?
- Can you think of a time when you might have let a friend down? Did you manage to make things up again?
- Would you be able to forgive a friend if they:

    a. Borrowed a CD from you and lost it?

    b. Didn't turn up at the cinema to see a film with you as agreed, but went to someone else's party instead without telling you?

    c. Told someone else the secret you had shared with them?

The rich man's gift

Story   There was once a rich man who had plenty of money, which, I guess, is why he was rich. He loved his riches, and liked nothing better than to count it all – his bags of coins, his bags of jewels, his ornaments of silver and gold. And when he'd finished counting it, he liked nothing better than to count it all over again.

One morning, as the rich man was counting his riches, he thought to himself, 'I am so lucky having all this money and all these jewels and all these precious ornaments. The very least I can do is to give a gift to the king. It must, of course, be something wonderful, something magnificent, something to make the king really take notice.'

So the rich man went off and thought for a while as to what this wonderful, magnificent gift could be. 'I know,' he said, 'I know, I shall have a wonderful statue made for the king. Perhaps a statue of a magnificent animal, all made in gold. I know the very thing: I shall have a statue made of an elephant, a huge, golden elephant.'

And the rich man smiled a broad smile.

But the smile did not last long. 'Hang on,' he thought to himself. 'Hang on, now let me think. Just how much gold would it take to make a golden elephant? Quite a lot, I'm sure.'

And when he thought of his gold and how much he liked it, the rich man decided on another plan. 'Perhaps something smaller would be better, smaller but no less regal of course. Instead of an elephant, what about a horse, a fine, noble, golden horse? Ah yes, the very thing.'

And the rich man smiled a broad smile. But the smile did not last long.

'Hang on,' he thought to himself. 'Hang on, now let me think. Just how much gold would it take to make a golden horse? Quite a lot I'm sure.' And when he thought of his gold and how much he liked it, the rich man decided on another plan.

'Perhaps something smaller would be better; smaller but no less impressive of course. Instead of a horse, what about a dog, a fine hunting dog? Ah, yes, the very thing.'

And the rich man smiled a broad smile. But the smile did not last long. 'Hang on,' he thought to himself. 'Hang on, now let me think. Just how much gold would it take to make a golden dog? Quite a lot, I'm sure.'

And when he thought of his gold and how much he liked it, the rich man decided on another plan.

'Perhaps something smaller would be better; smaller but no less attractive of course. Instead of a dog, what about a cat, a fine, sleek cat? Ah, yes, the very thing.'

And the rich man smiled a broad smile. But the smile did not last long.

'Hang on,' he thought to himself. 'Hang on, now let me think. Just how much gold would it take to make a golden cat? Quite a lot I'm sure.' And when he thought of his gold and how much he liked it, the rich man decided on another plan.

'Perhaps something smaller would be better, smaller but no less appealing of course. Instead of a cat what about a mouse, a cute little mouse? Ah, yes, the very thing.'

And the rich man smiled a broad smile and hurried off to see the jeweller straightaway. 'I would like you to make me a wonderful golden statue of a mouse – with diamonds for its eyes. It is to be a present for the king, no less.'

The jeweller set to work almost immediately and it was not long before he had completed the statue. But when he saw it, the rich man did not smile broadly at all. Instead he shook his head. 'Dear, dear, dear, you have used an awful lot of gold for this statue.' And when he picked it up, he exclaimed to the jeweller, 'This statue is very heavy!'

'That's because it is solid gold'

'Solid gold!' said the rich man. 'Solid gold, is that really necessary? Perhaps you could hollow it out, there is no need to go quite so far with it all. Oh, and while we are at it, I think the diamond eyes are perhaps a little excessive. Perhaps you could just paint them on, that would do.'

And so the rich man's hollow statue of a mouse with painted eyes was ready for the king.

The rich man prepared to set off for the palace but before he went, he thought to himself, 'I can't leave all my money and gold and jewels and precious ornaments here whilst I am away, they are much too precious. I must take them with me.'

And so the rich man loaded his riches on the back of five donkeys and set off to the palace.

The journey to the palace was a very wet one. It rained and it rained as a storm began to brew. The wind blew and the trees creaked and groaned as they were blown from side to side. As quickly as he could with the five donkeys, the rich man hurried over the thin bridge that led to the castle.

The guards at the gates let the rich man through and he hurried inside the palace out of the wind and the rain. 'Your Majesty,' said the rich man, bowing low. 'I have travelled all this way to bring you a gift, a gift paid for all by myself.'

'Why, thank you,' said the king graciously. 'May I see it?'

'It is here, Your Majesty, your very own statue of a . . . mouse.'

'I see,' said the king, 'that is very kind indeed. I do not think that I have ever had a hollow statue of a mouse before. I shall put it on my mantelpiece and it will always remind me of you. And of course,' said the king, 'you must stay as my guest and enjoy some food and drink.'

But the rich man had other plans; he was keen to get home. He knew that there was one bag of money which he had left under his mattress at home, and he was anxious to get back and count all the coins inside it. 'I'm afraid, Your Majesty,' he said, 'that I must set off at once. I have a very pressing engagement that I must attend to.'

'But you can't set off now,' protested the king. 'Look at the dreadful weather! There is a nasty storm blowing out there, please stay inside where it is warm and dry.'

But the rich man thought anxiously about his bag of money under his mattress. 'No, no,' he said. 'I'm afraid I really do have to go.' And he did.

But when he stepped outside, he saw to his horror that the thin bridge had been blown so violently by the raging wind that it had split in two and he could no longer cross it.

'This is dreadful!' said the rich man, 'I just have to get home.'

A smile spread across his face when he saw a small rowing boat down by the side of the river. Battling against the wind and the rain, he dragged the boat into the water and then began to fill it with the bags from his five donkeys. He didn't seem to worry, or perhaps he didn't notice, that the boat sank lower and lower in the water as he piled on more and more bags. Eventually, with the last of the bags on board, the rich man himself climbed in and began the treacherous journey across the wild river.

But the raging water swirled and churned, rocking the boat this way and that until the rich man tumbled out and down into the dark water.

'Help!' called the rich man pitifully. 'Help!' as he felt himself being dragged helplessly under.

Suddenly, a shout went up from the castle and there was a splash as a figure dived into the water. It was the prince, the king's son. He swam towards the rich man, and with a huge effort managed to drag him to the bank at the far side of the river. The king reached out his hand and helped to drag the rich man out.

As the rich man lay panting and exhausted the king said simply, 'There is no need to worry. You are saved.'

'But what about my money? The important thing is, what has happened to all of that money?' said the rich man sadly as he was led back to the castle.

General theme

What are our priorities? The things that we think are very important?

The rich man in the story had decided what was important to him – his money. It affected every decision he made. It meant he wasn't even prepared to give the king a proper gift. But in the end, his concern for his money – his priorities – put him in real danger. The king had very different priorities. He was concerned about other people. So concerned, he was prepared to risk everything – even his son – to try and save the rich man. What are our priorities? Are we too concerned about ourselves and our possessions? Or, do we think and care about others?

Christian theme

We all have different priorities, things that are important to us. The rich man in the story was interested only in his money. It meant everything to him. So much so that he wasn't even prepared to give a proper gift to the king. In the end his priorities put him in real danger.

The Bible talks a lot about priorities. It explains how important it is for our priorities to be about people and not just about ourselves and our possessions. The Bible tells us that we are such a high priority for God that he was prepared to offer everything to us – even his own Son: 'He did not spare his own Son, but gave him up for us all.' (Romans 8:32)

PSHME ideas

This story can be used to discuss:

- Values
- Priorities
- Selfishness
- Self-sacrifice
- Greed

- What are the most important things in your life?

- If you had been given £20 as a birthday present, and someone you hardly knew said they needed it desperately, would you give it all to them?

- If you had no money to buy anything with, which of your possessions would you give as a present to a king?

- How much money would you need to make you really happy?

The tailor and the apple tree

Story There was once a tailor who lived a comfortable life with his wife and children in a pretty little cottage with a pretty little garden. Though the cottage was not very big, there was certainly enough room for the whole family. The fires in the fire-place kept them warm in the winter and the garden was always a delight in summer.

The tailor particularly enjoyed working in his garden and he would grow the most beautiful flowers in his flower-beds, some of which he would place in vases to brighten the house. He also grew tasty vegetables in the vegetable patch, which the family loved to eat. The tailor also had an apple tree in the middle of his garden, and it was this one thing that spoiled his happy life.

Now, although the apple tree was covered in beautiful white blossom in early spring and produced fruit later in the year, the apples were never very big or round or red or sweet. And no matter what the tailor did, it was always the same. That was bad enough, but there was something that made it worse.

In the cottage next door, there lived an old woman called Mrs Miller. Now Mrs Miller also had an apple tree in her garden. Just like the tailor's, her tree was always covered in blossom in spring. But later in the year when the apples appeared, they always looked magnificent – so full and red and round and sweet. Indeed, the tailor sometimes imagined that he could almost taste how sweet the apples were on Mrs Miller's tree, but when he looked at his own apples it made him sad.

The tailor, since it was his job, spent his days hard at work sewing and mending and making all sorts of fine clothes, and each evening he would return home where his wife would have made a wonderful meal. She was a fantastic cook but the thing she made the best was apple pie – delicious apple pie. As a special treat, each Friday she would bake a large apple pie. And as he walked along the path to the cottage in the evening, the tailor could smell the delicious aroma of apple pie drifting towards him. 'Hmm, wonderful!'

Hungrily, he sat down to a very large slice of pie and, turning to his wife, the tailor said, 'My dear, I don't know how you manage it, for the apples on our tree always look rather small and not very tasty, but your pie is so sweet and delicious.'

'Well, it's like this, my dear . . .' said his wife.

But the tailor interrupted her. 'No, no, I don't want to know your secret; it would somehow spoil it all for me.' And instead, he settled down and took a very large mouthful of pie – it really was delicious!

That weekend, the tailor worked hard in his garden and he couldn't help noticing Mrs Miller's apple tree with its wonderful round, red, ripe apples, and he couldn't help noticing the rather pathetic looking apples on his tree.

'It's just not fair,' he thought, 'not fair at all.' And the more he looked at the apples on Mrs Miller's tree, the angrier he became.

But by Friday he was in a much better mood, for as he made his way home, he could smell the wonderful aroma of apple pie – his wife's fantastic apple pie.

As he sat down to a particularly large slice he said, 'This is magnificent my dear, I really don't know how you can take our rather small apples and make such a delicious tasting pie.'

'Well, you see . . .' began his wife.

But the tailor was quick to interrupt. 'No, no, dear, don't tell me. Good cooks always keep the secrets of their recipes.' And he happily helped himself to another slice of pie.

That weekend, the tailor was busy again working in his garden and busy looking at the apple tree in Mrs Miller's garden. 'Now how can she have such a wonderful apple tree and with such big, ripe apples and mine are so small. It's just not fair!' And the more he thought about it, the angrier he became. So angry that he stamped about his garden, scowling and mumbling to himself.

Luckily, by Friday he had calmed down and was able to enjoy the apple pie that his wife had made. 'You truly are a marvel my dear, I can't believe there is anyone in all the world who can make an apple pie as well as you. I just don't know how you do it.'

'Well, it's easy my dear . . .' his wife began.

'No, no, don't tell me,' said the tailor with his mouth full of apple pie. 'Remember. Good cooks never reveal their secrets.'

But the next day, the tailor was in his garden looking over the fence at Mrs Miller's apple tree and muttering angrily to himself. 'Why should she have all the luck and have an apple tree with such perfect apples? She doesn't deserve it!'

And the more he thought about it and looked at the apples on his tree, the angrier he became, so angry that he came up with a plan. He decided that he would have to destroy Mrs Miller's tree. He rubbed his hands together in satisfaction. 'What an excellent idea!' he thought to himself.

The tailor waited until it grew dark, and when his wife and children were safely asleep in bed, he sneaked downstairs and out into his shed. There he began to mix together a potion of powders and water. The liquid seemed to hiss and steam as he carried it out of the shed in an old tin watering can.

Quietly, as quietly as he could, the tailor climbed over the fence and tiptoed his way towards Mrs Miller's tree. And then he poured the potion he had mixed all over the roots of the tree. He could almost hear it hiss and bubble as it soaked into the ground. With a cruel smile, the tailor made his way back over the fence and then crept into his cottage.

Sure enough, the very next day, when the tailor looked over the fence at Mrs. Miller's apple tree, he saw that the leaves were no longer green and healthy, but were dark brown and dry. Within a week, the apples and leaves had all dropped off and the branches drooped terribly. And when he looked at the tree, the tailor was very happy.

The next Friday the tailor returned home in a very good mood. It felt wonderful not having to think about Mrs Miller's apple tree any more. And when he saw his favourite apple pie there on the table he was happier than ever.

Until he took a bite.

The tailor wrinkled his nose in disgust. 'My dear, what on earth is this? Your apple pie is usually delicious, but I'm afraid this is far from that. What has happened? I can't eat this.'

'I'm sorry, my dear,' his wife exclaimed sadly, 'but there's nothing I can do. It's all to do with the secret of my pies, which you have asked me not to tell you. Well, today I will have to. The pies I have made for you in the past have been so good because the apples came from Mrs Miller's tree. She had been happy enough to give us apples from her tree for she had more than enough, and she had taken some of ours in exchange to feed to her pigs. But I'm afraid something dreadful happened to her tree and it is dead and has been cut down. And now she can't give us any more apples to make my apple pie. The only apples we have left are the ones on our tree, so what the pigs used to enjoy will now have to do for us.'

The tailor put down his spoon and did not eat any more of his apple pie. And he has not eaten another since.

General theme

I wonder if you've ever thought, 'I wish I had what he's got' or 'That's not fair, she's got more than me'? And then you get so concerned with what someone else has that you can't enjoy what you have. That's what happened to the poor tailor in the story. All he could think about was the apple tree in the garden next door. And the more he thought about it, the more cross it made him feel. He couldn't even enjoy the fact that he was lucky enough to have a tree of his own, or enjoy the magnificent apple pie that his wife made for him. And the more he thought, the worse his anger got. He got so cross, it was as if he couldn't see clearly; he was blind to everything else around him. In the end, the only thing he could think of doing was to destroy what Mrs Miller had.

But actually, it didn't make him feel better – it made things worse when he realised that he had been enjoying the apples from her tree all that time. The tailor's bad feeling started off as just a tiny thought, but it grew and it grew and led to disaster.

I hope we are wise enough to stop such things happening when we see what other people might have.

Christian theme

From the smallest things all sorts of problems can grow. The tailor's problems started from just a small thought, a bit of jealousy over an apple tree. But the more he thought about it, the more the problem seemed to grow and grow; so much so that he couldn't think properly, he couldn't enjoy the good things that he had and in the end it led him to want to destroy what Mrs Miller had. He just couldn't be content with what he had.

In the Bible, Paul was shipwrecked, imprisoned, even beaten by soldiers but he was able to say, 'I am content in all things' (Philippians 4:12). It seems very strange: what did he have to be content about? He didn't have lots of possessions, in fact things seemed to be very difficult for him. But he had a strong faith in God and that made him content. It meant so much more to him than the possessions he had, or the possessions someone else had.

I wonder where we find our contentment?

PSHME ideas

This story can be used to discuss:
* Contentment
* Jealousy
* Possessions
* Envy

- How many times today have you said, 'I want . . .'?
- How many times this week have you thought, 'I wish I had . . .'?
- How much money would it take for you to feel really contented?
- Do you always have to spend money to get contentment?
- How long does it take for you to become bored with your Christmas presents?

The two brothers

Story　There were once two brothers called Tom and Jack. They were both hardworking and lived in a small cottage together with their mother and father. Now, whilst they were brothers and many people said how alike they looked, they were as different as chalk and cheese; for Tom was a very generous person . . . and Jack was . . . well, let us just say that Jack was not.

Although the two brothers worked hard each day, helping on the family farm, both knew they wanted something more. Tom and Jack both had an ambition that, one day, they would travel to the Grand City, where the royal palace stood, and see the king himself.

One evening, after the two brothers had spent a hard day working in the fields, they sat resting by the fire. Tom turned to Jack and said, 'You know Jack, I think the time has come for us to try to get to the city where the palace stands.'

'I think you're right,' Jack replied. 'For if we don't go soon, we will never go; we will spend the rest of our years sowing and weeding and harvesting and never have time to make it to the city or to see the king.'

And so, as they sat there relaxing by the fire, they decided that the very next morning they would set out on their journey.

When the two brothers awoke the next day, they packed together a few things into a tight bundle. 'We will need to take the donkeys with us,' said Tom to Jack, 'just to help carry our bundles.'

'And to carry me, if the going gets tough,' said Jack who was already pulling the two rather reluctant donkeys out from their small stable. They loaded their things onto the donkeys and set off along the road, waving goodbye to their mother and father as they went.

It wasn't long before they met an old woman who was struggling along carrying some very heavy bundles of firewood. Jack and Tom stopped. 'Dear me,' said Tom, 'this will never do, there must be something we can do to help.'

'I don't see how,' said Jack as he lay back against his donkey. 'Besides, I'm sure she hasn't got far to go and those bundles probably aren't that heavy.'

But Tom was not to be put off. 'Let me help you, Madam, you can't carry a heavy load like that on your own! You need help; why not take my donkey? He's strong and he'll be able to carry all those bundles for you.'

The old lady was overjoyed. 'Thank you,' she said, 'oh, thank you, that is wonderful! I'm afraid I have very little to repay your kindness, but here, please take a bundle of firewood.' And she handed one to Tom.

And then she looked at Jack. 'And here's one for you too.'

'Oh, ta,' said Jack.

So Tom set off carrying his bundle of firewood and Jack followed behind with his donkey and his bag of clothes and his bundle of firewood.

It wasn't long before they passed a small boy who was busy digging up potatoes and putting them into sacks. The poor boy looked very cold and he shivered as he worked.

'Oh dear, dear, dear,' said Tom, 'this will never do, there must be something we can do to help.'

'I don't see how,' said Jack as he lay back against his donkey. 'Besides, I'm sure he isn't really all that cold.'

But Tom was not to be put off. 'Here, let me help you. What you need is a nice warm fire and I have a bundle of firewood which will do the trick. Here, you can have it.'

'Thank you,' said the poor boy. 'Oh, thank you, that is wonderful. I'm afraid I have very little to repay your kindness, but here, please take a sack of potatoes.' And he handed one to Tom.

And then he looked at Jack. 'And here's one for you too.'

'Oh, ta,' said Jack.

So Tom set off carrying his sack of potatoes and Jack followed behind with his donkey and his bag of clothes and his bundle of firewood and his sack of potatoes.

As they travelled along it wasn't long before they met a builder working on a house. And though he worked, he looked terribly thin and hungry.

'Oh dear, dear, dear,' said Tom, 'this will never do, there must be something we can do to help.'

'I don't see how,' said Jack as he lay back against his donkey. 'Besides, I'm sure he isn't really all that hungry.'

But Tom was not to be put off. 'Here, let me help you. What you need is something good to eat, some nourishing soup. I have just the thing. These potatoes will make a really hearty soup. Here, you must take this sack.'

'Why, thank you,' said the hungry builder. 'Thank you, that is marvellous. I'm afraid I have very little to repay your kindness, but here, please take some of these stones.'

And he handed some to Tom.

And then he looked at Jack. 'And here's some for you too.'

'Oh, ta,' said Jack.

So Tom set off carrying his pile of stones and Jack followed slowly behind, with his donkey and his bag of clothes and his bundle of firewood and his sack of potatoes and his pile of stones.

Before they had gone very far at all, they met a shepherd standing by the side of the road. He was looking at a hole in the side of his sheep pen.

'This is dreadful,' said the shepherd, 'I need to repair that wall or my sheep will escape but I have nothing to use.' And he shook his head sadly.

'Oh dear, dear, dear,' said Tom, 'this will never do, there must be something we can do to help.'

'I don't see how,' said Jack as he lay back against his donkey. 'Besides, I'm sure he'll be able to find something.'

But Tom was not to be put off. 'Here, let me help you. What you need is something solid to help repair your wall; I have some stones that would be perfect. Here, you must take these.'

'Why, thank you,' said the shepherd, 'thank you, that is marvellous. I'm afraid I have very little to repay your kindness but here, please take one of these sheep.'

And he handed one to Tom.

And then he looked at Jack. 'And here's one for you too.'

'Oh, ta,' said Jack.

So Tom set off leading his sheep and Jack followed very slowly behind with his donkey and his bag of clothes and his bundle of firewood and his sack of potatoes and his pile of stones and his sheep.

Eventually, Tom – and Jack, with his donkey and his bag of clothes and his bundle of firewood and his sack of potatoes and his pile of stones and his sheep – arrived at the Grand City, and through the gateway they could see the imposing building of the king's palace.

'Wow, this is it!' said Tom, turning to Jack. 'At last, the moment we have always dreamed of – just through these gates and we will get to the palace and maybe meet the king.'

And Tom set off through the gateway with his sheep, towards the palace. And Jack followed for a few steps at least.

But as he tried to squeeze his way through the gateway with his donkey and his bag of clothes and his bundle of firewood and his sack of potatoes and his pile of stones and his sheep, he got stuck . . . stuck so tight that he couldn't move. Not forwards or backwards . . . stuck fast.

And I'm told if you go to the Grand City today you can still see Jack wedged in the gateway with all his things keeping him trapped as tight as can be.

General theme

I wonder how much time we spend thinking about what we can have: 'I want this! I want that!' 'Let me have it! It's mine!' Perhaps you've heard other people say things like that . . . or perhaps you've even heard yourself saying it! Tom was given so many different things, but rather than keeping them to himself like Jack did, he was happy to share them to help make a difference to somebody else.

Jack, meanwhile, clung on tightly to everything he'd got . . . but it didn't do him any good in the end.

Do we take the chance to see how we can help others? Are we ready to share or do we really care only about ourselves?

Christian theme

After all that journeying there was only one of the two brothers who got to see the king. Poor old Jack got left behind, stuck with all the things he gathered and kept to himself, wedged tight in the gate.

Tom managed to see the king; but not only that, he managed to help plenty of other people as well on his journey, and made a real difference to their lives.

Even though we have so much, we are often tempted, like Jack, to cling on to it. But Jesus says we should be ready to make a difference, by thinking not just about ourselves but about others too. He said, 'Freely you have received, freely you should give.' (Matthew 10:8)

We each have something we can share, maybe it is our time or our friendship . . . but are we ready to make a difference, are we ready to give?

PSHME ideas

This story can be used to discuss:

- Possessions
- Generosity
- Sharing
- Selfishness

- If you won the lottery, would you give any of it away? If so, to whom?
- If you were given £5, would you give any of it away? If so, to whom?
- And what if you were given £1?
- If you had £2 and you had to give it away, would you give it to:
  a. Your Mum, so she could buy herself a present?
  b. Your friend, so they could buy a book they've always wanted?
  c. A charity collecting box for a donkey sanctuary?
  d. A stranger who had lost their bus fare home?
- How easy would it be to give 10 minutes a day to helping someone?

Cedric and the beautiful garden

Story There was once a king who owned a magnificent palace, and all around the palace was the most amazing garden. It was full of brightly coloured flowers that smelt wonderful. There were beautiful trees and fruit orchards that swayed gently to and fro and seemed to play a magical tune whenever the wind blew through their leaves. There were wonderful lawns as green as emeralds.

The king really enjoyed his garden, but he also knew other people would too, so he opened them for all the villagers nearby to come and enjoy. The gardens were always full of people admiring the flowers and the trees or sitting quietly on the grass listening to the sound of the birds singing in the orchards.

One day, the king had to go on a long journey. 'What I need,' he said to himself, 'is someone who can look after my garden for me. Someone sensible, someone reliable, someone wise who can be trusted to do the right thing.'

'That's me,' said Cedric, one of the king's servants overhearing the king's words. 'I'm just the person you need. Oh yes, you can trust me. I'll make sure your garden is looked after superbly until your return. Don't you worry about a thing, just you leave it to me.'

So the king put Cedric in charge of his magnificent garden before setting off on his long journey.

Cedric was very excited. 'I just know I am going to do a wonderful job of looking after this garden,' he said. 'Oh yes, the king is going to be so proud of me.' And so saying, he sat down on the grass and looked up at the blue sky and listened to the birds singing.

But it wasn't long before Cedric said to himself, 'This is no good, this is much too hard. What I need is somewhere comfortable to sit. I need a bench, a nice wooden bench. Now where could I get some wood to make a bench?'

And he thought and he thought. 'Ah, hang on, the very thing,' he said looking around the orchard. 'Trees, the very thing if I need wood.'

And with his axe, Cedric began to chop down some trees to make a bench to sit on. It didn't take him long and when it was finished, Cedric was very pleased with it. 'Ah, this is perfect,' he said as he sat down on his new bench. 'I just know the king is going to be very happy. A nice new wooden bench which he can sit on and enjoy his magnificent garden.'

And Cedric sat down and enjoyed looking at the lovely green grass and the multicoloured flowers and listening to the birds singing.

But as Cedric sat there on his bench, he began to get a bit restless. 'You know, this bench is all very well and this garden is quite magnificent, but in a garden as magnificent as this, what you really need to be able to do is to sit back and enjoy a nice cool drink, but there is nowhere to put it. Now what I really need is a table, a nice wooden table. Now where could I get some wood to make a table?'

And he thought and he thought. 'Ah, hang on, the very thing,' he said looking around the orchard. 'Trees, the very thing if I need wood.'

And with his axe, Cedric began to chop down some trees to make a table to put his drink on. It didn't take him long and when it was finished, Cedric was very pleased with it.

'Ah, this is perfect,' he said as he sat on his bench and put a cool drink in a glass on his new table. 'I just know the king is going to be very happy with his nice new wooden bench and his nice new table to put his drinks on. He will really be able to enjoy his magnificent garden.'

And Cedric sat down on his bench and put a drink on his table; he sat back to enjoy looking at the lovely green grass and the multicoloured flowers and listening to the birds singing.

But as Cedric sat there it was not long before he became restless, really restless. 'Hmm, this bench is all very well for sitting on, and this table is fine for putting drinks on, but when the sun is shining down and the birds are singing and the flowers are waving gently in the breeze, what you really need to do to be able to relax is to lie down; to lie out nice and flat and rest. Now, what I really need is a . . . now, what are they called? . . . ah yes, a sunlounger. But if I am going to make a sunlounger, I'll need something to make it from. Now what on earth could I make it from?' And Cedric stood and thought, and thought.

'Wood!' he said suddenly, 'the very thing. I shall make my sunlounger from wood. But the problem is, where can I get wood from? That's a tricky one.'

And he looked this way and that around the garden until he suddenly said, 'Aha! The very thing! I can get wood from the trees in the orchard.'

And with his axe he began to chop down the remaining trees – all of them. And then he made his sunlounger. It didn't take long and when he was finished with it, Cedric was very pleased, very pleased indeed.

As he lay out on it, he thought to himself, 'This is magnificent, the king is going to be so pleased. He has a nice wooden bench to sit on to enjoy his garden, a lovely wooden table for his royal drinks and when the weather is warm, he can lie out on his new sunlounger and have a royal sunbathe. It's magnificent!'

But as Cedric lay there, he began to get restless, very restless. 'You know, there seems to be something missing. The bench is all very well for sitting on, and the table is fine for putting drinks on and the sunlounger is just perfect for reclining in the sun, but it's very difficult to really enjoy the flowers when they are so far away; there must be something I can do.'

And there was.

Cedric took hold of a shovel and dug up all the flowers and then found as many different vases as possible. He arranged them carefully on the table and all around the sunlounger and filled them with the flowers he had dug up.

'This is just perfect, said Cedric as he lay on the sunlounger and admired the flowers that were so close to him that he could reach out and touch them. 'The king is going to be overjoyed when he comes back, I just know it.'

At the end of the week, the king did return. After his long journey he was anxious to return to his palace and enjoy his magnificent gardens. He hurried up to the palace gates where he was greeted by Cedric.

Cedric gave a low bow. 'Your Majesty, what a pleasant surprise to see you. And I have a special surprise for you too,' he said with a smile.

'Oh, really?' said the king with interest.

'Yes,' Cedric continued. 'I'm quite sure you won't believe your eyes when you get to see what I have done to the royal gardens. You'll probably be speechless, at a loss for words.'

And he led the king round to see the magnificent gardens. 'Your Majesty, look at this bench, you will be so comfortable on it, and this table is just perfect for putting your drinks on. And this sunlounger is a must for those hot, sunny days. And look, Your Majesty, you don't even have to walk around your garden, I have brought the flowers to you.'

The king looked around him, at the missing orchard, the bare and empty flower beds and shook his head.

'Just as I suspected, Your Majesty, you are speechless.'

And indeed the king was . . . almost. All he managed to say was, 'Guards, take Cedric to the dungeons!'

General theme

What a responsibility Cedric had. The whole of the king's magnificent gardens to look after. The king thought he'd chosen the right man for the job, but unfortunately he was wrong. Far from looking after the garden, Cedric ended up almost destroying it in his attempts to come up with yet more things which would make his life, and eventually that of the king, a little easier – a seat so that he could feel just that little bit more comfortable, a table so his drink was easily within reach, a sunlounger so he could really lie out and enjoy the sun . . . but at what cost? We too have a great responsibility when we consider the world around us. There is so much beauty and many wonderful natural resources around, but we are often rather like Cedric, too ready to chop things down, or dig things up because we think it will make things easier for ourselves and a few others. We often have no real thought as to the effect of this behaviour on everybody else or on the natural world itself.

Sometimes we need to stop and take our responsibility seriously, or there may be very serious consequences to face.

Christian theme

Cedric was given a very special job, one of great responsibility: to look after the king's magnificent garden. But he turned out to be a poor choice. In the end he almost destroyed the king's garden, which meant no one else could enjoy it, not even the king himself. And all because Cedric wanted to make some things that would make life just that little bit more comfortable.

The Bible tells us how we have all been given a very special responsibility to care for the earth. And when we think of all the wonderful things there are in the natural world, that is a big responsibility.

If we are selfish and misuse natural resources simply to make things just that little bit more comfortable for ourselves, not only does it spoil the world, it betrays the trust God put in us. It also means we end up ignoring the needs of so many other people.

Does our attitude towards the world, even towards the environment around us, show we are responsible, or are we too much like Cedric?

PSHME ideas   This story can be used to discuss:

- The environment
- Responsibility
- Trust

- Imagine a cake that has been divided into ten slices. Do you think it would be fair for two people to share eight slices and eight people to share the remaining two slices? If we think of the earth's resources as being like this cake, how should they be shared? How do you think they are shared at the moment?
- Large areas of forests are cut down and cleared away every day – can you think of some reasons why people might feel they need to cut down forests?
- Imagine it is your job to clear the trees away from a large area of rain forest, what arguments would you give to support what you have to do?
- Imagine your family have lived in an area of forests for many years. You know the area is going to be cleared of all the trees. What arguments would you give for keeping the trees?
- Every person has the right to have a car – do you agree?

Farmer Joe

Story There was once a farmer called Joe who lived on a farm, as most farmers do. Farmer Joe was very proud of his farm. He had sheep and cows and pigs, and a wonderful farmhouse with a pretty thatched roof.

Every morning, Farmer Joe would get up, put his clothes on, pull on his wellington boots and head outside to see his animals.

First he would go and look at his sheep. 'Morning sheep,' said Farmer Joe as he looked over the fence – but the sheep didn't say anything back . . . well you wouldn't expect them to really, being sheep.

Next, Farmer Joe would walk over to his cows. 'Morning cows,' said Farmer Joe as he leant on the wall. But the cows never really said anything back either, apart from 'Moo', – well that's what you'd expect, they were cows after all.

And then Farmer Joe would go and see his pigs. 'Morning pigs,' said Farmer Joe as he looked into the sty – but the pigs didn't say anything, well they were only pigs.

And after a hard day's work on the farm, Farmer Joe would make his way back to his wonderful farmhouse with the pretty thatched roof.

One morning when Farmer Joe woke, he was certain he could smell something odd.

What was it? The smell of frying bacon? No. He sniffed again. The aroma of baking bread? No that wasn't it.

Hang on, he knew what it was: it was the smell of burning. Something was burning, something in his wonderful farmhouse with the pretty thatched roof.

Farmer Joe raced to the telephone and immediately dialled for the fire brigade. And before long the sound of the siren could be heard as the fire engine raced up the drive towards the wonderful farmhouse with the pretty thatched roof.

'Oh, I'm so glad you're here,' called Farmer Joe as a fireman rushed up to the doorway, unreeling a large hose as he went.

'Well, now I'm here there's no need to worry,' the fireman replied, 'I'll soon have the fire out.' And he raced inside with Farmer Joe right behind him.

'Mind, out of the way,' called the fireman, 'I can see where the trouble is!' and he threw open the door of the lounge and started to hurry in.

'Oh, no!' called Farmer Joe, suddenly. 'No, no, no, we don't go in there!'

'Whatever's the matter?' asked the fireman.

'I'll tell you what the matter is. I had a row with my brother Harold in there about pickled onions in 1954. Oh, a dreadful row it was, though I know I was right. He said all sorts of things to me and I've not forgiven him . . . no, we never go in there, so out you come.'

And Farmer Joe pulled the fireman out and closed the door.

'But the room's on fire,' the fireman protested, 'I need to put it out!'

'Well, you're not going in there, not after what my brother said to me about pickled onions. I've not forgiven him. You'll have to try somewhere else.'

'OK,' said the fireman, 'I'll try in here.' And he raced towards the kitchen where he was sure he could hear flames. He threw open the kitchen door.

'Oh, no!' called Farmer Joe, suddenly. 'No, no, no, we don't go in there!'

'Whatever's the matter?' asked the fireman.

'I'll tell you what the matter is. I had a row in there with my sister Enid in 1963 about who made the best pastry. A dreadful row it was, though I know that my pastry was the best. Oh, she said some hurtful things about my pastry and I've never forgiven her, never. So we don't go in there.'

And Farmer Joe pulled the fireman out and closed the door.

'But hang on,' called the fireman, 'the house is on fire and I need to put it out.'

'I know the house is on fire,' said Farmer Joe. 'You don't have to tell me that. I was the one who called you, remember.'

'But what can I do?' said the fireman. 'I can't go in the lounge 'cause you had a row with your brother Harold about pickled onions and I can't go in the kitchen because you had a row with your sister Enid about pastry, so where can I go?'

'Well, couldn't you try upstairs?' suggested Farmer Joe.

'OK,' said the fireman and he raced up the stairs dragging his hose behind him. 'Aha, there's plenty of smoke up here. If I work fast I might be able to stop the flames spreading and setting light to your pretty thatched roof,' and he raced to the bedroom door and hurried inside.

'Oh, no!' called Farmer Joe, suddenly. 'No, no, no, we don't go in there!'

'Whatever's the matter?' asked the fireman.

'I'll tell you what the matter is. I had a row with my cousin Betty in there in 1967 about the colour of the curtains. A dreadful row it was, though I know I was right about having blue. Oh, she said some hurtful things about me and my curtains and I've not forgiven her, never. So we don't go in there!' And Farmer Joe pulled the Fireman out and closed the door.

'But wait a minute,' he protested, 'this is silly. Don't you understand that your house is on fire?'

'I know my house is on fire,' said Farmer Joe, 'You don't have to tell me that. I was the one that called you, remember.'

'But what can I do?' said the fireman. 'I can't go in the lounge 'cause you had a row with your brother Harold about pickled onions and I can't go in the kitchen because you had a row with your sister Enid about pastry, and I can't go in the bedroom because you had a row with your cousin Betty about the curtains; so where can I go?'

'Well, couldn't you just squirt your hose around a bit outside? I've never had a row there.'

And he led the fireman outside into the yard. 'Here you go, you can squirt it here.' So the fireman did.

'Right, well thank you very much for coming,' said Farmer Joe as he waved goodbye to the very confused fireman.

But when Farmer Joe turned back to his wonderful farmhouse with its pretty thatched roof, he saw that it was burning wildly and even as he stood watching, it fell to the ground with a loud and smoky crash, till all that was left of the wonderful farmhouse with the pretty thatched roof was a small smouldering pile.

'Oh dear,' said Farmer Joe shaking his head, 'now that *is* a blow, there's something just not right that's happened here, though I can't for the life of me work out quite what went wrong.'

General theme Sometimes people say that 'sorry' is one of the hardest words to say. Perhaps it is because if we say sorry, we have to admit that we were wrong, and we can sometimes find that hard. But there is another side to 'Sorry'. If people say they are sorry we need to be ready to forgive them. And forgiving can seem very hard to do as well. Farmer Joe really struggled with forgiving people. He had had rows with his brother and his sister and his cousin and just couldn't forgive them. After all those years he still kept thinking about it, and in the end it made him behave in such a ridiculous way that he was the person who lost out. To forgive someone means to be ready to give them another chance, to be ready to accept them. Sometimes that is hard if they have really upset us; but to hold on to our anger and our resentment can prove to be even worse: not only does it destroy relationships, it can hurt us just as badly.

Have we the courage not only to say sorry when we need to, but also to forgive?

Christian theme

Poor Farmer Joe, what a ridiculous way to behave. We'd never be so silly, or would we? Whilst it is often hard to say sorry, it can also be very hard to forgive. Saying sorry means we have to admit we are wrong and that can be hard to do, but forgiving someone, really forgiving them, means accepting them and being ready to try again, even though it might not always work out right in the future.

The Bible tells how God is always ready to forgive people. Jesus, even at the most desperate time in his life, when the soldiers were nailing him to a cross, forgave them and asked God to forgive them too: 'Father, forgive them, for they don't know what they are doing' (Luke 23:34). In the Lord's Prayer we say, 'Forgive us our sins as we forgive those who sin against us'; not only is it a way for the person praying to say sorry, but it also shows that we need to be ready to forgive other people. It is only then that positive relationships can be restored and maintained. Holding on to our anger and not forgiving can lead to things festering and building up and up and lead us to do the most ridiculous things.

I wonder if you can face the challenge of forgiving someone today?

PSHME ideas

This story can be used to discuss:

- Forgiveness
- Openness

- Can you think of something that someone might do that you could never forgive them for?
- Can you think of a time when you found it almost impossible to forgive someone?
- How does it make you feel when you know someone should say sorry to you, but they don't?
- Have you ever had to say sorry to someone? How did it make you feel?

Two ugly bugs

Story   Down at the bottom of a deep, dark pond lived two ugly bugs, one big and one small.

The big ugly bug and the little ugly bug spent their time crawling about in the dark mud at the bottom of the pond looking for tiny scraps of things to eat.

One morning the little ugly bug looked up from the mud and said, 'Have you ever wondered what it's like up there, higher up in the pond, away from the bottom? Why do we have to be down here in the dark all the time?'

'Well, that's obvious,' said the big ugly bug, 'we've always lived here. It's always been like this, so this is the way it has to stay.'

But the little ugly bug shook his head in disagreement. 'No, there's got to be something different to all this crawling about in the mud. I'm sure there is and I'm going to find out.' And so saying, he crawled over to a clump of reeds that grew up from the bottom of the pond and began to crawl up one of the slender stems.

It was very tricky and several times his legs slithered and slipped, but he kept going and managed to make his way up, up, up.

And what a sight he was greeted with as he clung to the stem of the reed. Up here the water seemed so much clearer and he could see fish darting this way and that, their silver bodies flashing like jewels. It was amazing, something he had never seen before.

The little ugly bug called down into the dark water below to the big ugly bug. 'Why don't you come on up? It's amazing – there is so much to see up here!'

But the big ugly bug called back from the dark mud at the bottom of the pond, 'I'm not coming up, it's unnatural. We've always lived down here. It's always been like this, so this is the way it has to stay,' and he carried on searching for scraps in the mud.

The little ugly bug called down, 'Oh, go on, why not give it a go?'

'No, no, no,' replied and big ugly bug. 'Never!'

The little ugly bug clung tightly to his reed and peered up. Above him things seemed to be even brighter and clearer and he was determined to get higher. And so he clambered and slithered and slipped and climbed higher and higher up the reed.

As he climbed, he saw out of the corner of his eye a large fish racing towards him with its mouth wide open. The little ugly bug, terrified, clung tightly to the reed and tried to look as small as possible. With one final thrash of its tail, the fish gave a sudden turn and shot off in the other direction, leaving the little ugly bug holding on tightly to the reed. Cautiously, the little ugly bug continued his climbing. When he looked around he saw all sorts of things. He watched as a bright green frog swam by, kicking with its powerful legs. He could see the underside of large lily pads floating on the surface of the water above. And as he peered up, he could see the round red sun shining down brightly. The little ugly bug called down into the dark water below to the big ugly bug. 'Why don't you come on up? It's wonderful, there is so much to see.'

But the big ugly bug called back from the dark mud at the bottom of the pond, 'I'm not coming up, it's dangerous. We've always lived down here. It's always been like this, so this is the way it has to stay,' and he carried on searching for scraps in the mud.

The little ugly bug called down, 'Oh, go on, why not give it a go?'

'No, not on your Nelly,' replied the big ugly bug. 'Never!'

So, looking up, the little ugly bug continued his crawling. Up the stem of the reed he went, until at last he crawled right up and out of the pond.

As he clung to the top of the reed that swayed gently in the breeze he could see flowers of different colours all around the edge of the pond. And above him in the blue sky, birds swooped and soared. And high above, the sun shone bright and warm.

The little ugly bug called down into the pond, excitedly. 'Come on up, come on up, it's fantastic.'

But the big ugly bug simply called back, 'I'm not coming up there, it's far too tiring. We've always lived down here. It's always been like this, so this is the way that it has to stay,' and he carried on searching and scrabbling around for scraps in the dark mud at the bottom of the pond.

The little ugly bug called down again. 'Oh, go on, why not give it a go?'

'No, not in a million years,' replied the big ugly bug. 'Never!' After all his climbing, the little ugly bug felt very tired. More tired than he had ever been and as he felt the warm sun on his back he began to fall asleep.

He must have been exhausted, for he slept and he slept. When he finally awoke, the little ugly bug felt very strange, very strange indeed, not quite himself at all.

He stretched and he wriggled. His body felt different, almost new – and as he stretched again, on his back a pair of glistening fragile wings spread out. As they caught the sunlight they glistened like jewels. With a flap, he was off, swooping over the pond. And as he caught sight of his reflection he saw a beautiful turquoise-blue dragonfly.

With a huge smile on his face, he called down into the water to the big ugly bug. 'Come on up, come on up, you just won't believe what has happened.'

But the big ugly bug simply called back, 'I'm not coming up there, everything's different. We've always lived down here. It's always been like this, so this is the way that it has to stay,' and he carried on searching and scrabbling around for scraps in the dark mud at the bottom of the pond.

The little dragonfly called back down, 'Oh, go on, why not give it a go?'

'No, not in a million years,' replied the big ugly bug. 'Never, I'm staying here in the mud!'

General theme

'It's always been like this, so this is the way it has to stay'. That's what the big ugly bug thought. But he was wrong, there was another way. It took courage and effort for the little bug to decide to move away from where he had always been; to make a difference in his life. But what a difference, what a transformation!

Do we have the courage to make the effort to change, to see how we could make things so much better, or do we spend life like the big ugly bug, living in the dark and the muck, certain that nothing can ever change?

Christian theme

The big ugly bug thought things could never change, that he had to stay the way he was – 'that's the way it has always been, so that's the way it will always be.' Even though he was living in the muck and the gloom, he felt he couldn't change and be different. The little bug showed that he could.

Sometimes we can have the same attitude as the big ugly bug and think that we can never change, but the Bible says we can change, we can be a 'new creation' (2 Corinthians 5:17). We don't have to be a prisoner to what we used to be like, we can be set free to be different, to be changed and enjoy something better.

We can be like the little bug or we can be like the big one; there's the challenge . . . which are you like?

PSHME ideas   This story can be used to discuss:

- Change
- Determination
- Perseverance
- Challenge

- Can you think of any 'bad' habits that you have? Have you ever tried to break them? What did you do? How did you get on?
- Can you think of any 'good' habits that you have?
- What do you think the expression, 'You can't teach an old dog new tricks,' means?
- Do you agree with the expression, 'A leopard can't change its spots'?

Simon, swiftest sword this side of Swainsford

Story   There was once a bold fellow by the name of Simon. Simon was a royal musketeer, one of the king's own special band of elite soldiers, or so he said.

One morning, Simon set off to make a journey to the village because he needed to buy some things at the market.

His journey took him through a dark and rather foreboding wood. But Simon was not worried for, after all, he was a musketeer.

As he travelled through the wood, Simon suddenly felt that he was being followed. Nervously he looked around. 'Who . . . who . . . goes there?' he called with a slight shake in his voice.

'It is I,' came a loud reply, and stepping out from behind the trees stood a tall fellow with a sword at his side.

'Good morning to you, Sir,' said the stranger bowing low to Simon. 'My name is Roderick, and whom do I have the pleasure of meeting in this dark, foreboding wood?'

Simon bowed in return before answering rather proudly. 'I, Sir, am a musketeer: Simon, swiftest sword this side of Swainsford.'

'Then I am most honoured to meet you, Simon – swiftest sword this side of Swainsford,' said Roderick. 'This is a real stroke of luck, a real-life musketeer. I have always wanted to be a musketeer. It has been my life's ambition. I have often heard about how brave and dedicated they are and how loyal they are to the king. If you have time as we walk along together in this dark, foreboding wood, perhaps you wouldn't mind answering a few questions for me?'

'Why, of course,' replied Simon. 'Anything at all.'

'Well then, Simon, swiftest sword this side of Swainsford, I feel that I am quite a swordsman myself, but to be a musketeer just how good would I need to be?'

'You would need to practise every day,' replied Simon. 'Every day without fail. Take a leaf from my book, I practise my sword skills every day . . . except for yesterday, because the weather wasn't too good.' Simon hesitated, 'And the day before as well, come to that. In fact, come to think of it, I didn't get to do much sword-skill practising at all last week, what with friends coming round and one thing and another. Still, I have got some time pencilled in for next week . . . though that might clash with the gardening, if the weather picks up.' Roderick looked slightly confused but Simon added, 'But no matter, for I am still a musketeer!' Roderick and Simon continued their way through the dark, foreboding wood, heading towards the village.

And Roderick continued with his eager questions. 'My sword is pretty sharp, but I bet yours is amazing, Simon, swiftest sword this side of Swainsford – truly formidable. Can I see it?'

'Why of course,' said Simon and he reached down to his side. 'Hang on,' he said looking at his empty belt, 'um, I don't think I've got it with me today. Now where's that gone? Oh yes, I remember, it's by the fireplace back at home. I was using it as a toasting fork. But not to worry, because I do have a dagger with me and that can be a lethal weapon in the right hands. Let me show you.' And he reached inside his pocket and pulled out his . . . handkerchief.

'Now that is odd,' said Simon, 'I was sure I'd got my dagger. Hold on, I must have something here,' and he rummaged further in his pockets. 'Aha,' he said, 'I might not have my dagger, but what I do have is this . . . a toothpick,' and he brandished it in the air above his head. 'And no matter, for I am still a musketeer.'

Roderick did not look that convinced, 'That is indeed a strange weapon for a musketeer, Simon, swiftest toothpick this side of Swainsford, but I'm sure you must know what you are doing. Now, I do not wish to appear rude but I had imagined that a musketeer would be dressed in fine clothes, a special sort of uniform.'

'Yes, the musketeer has a special uniform, let me assure you of that,' Simon said hastily. 'There is the special hat with a fine, long feather, which adorns it, and an embroidered, velvet cape.'

'I suppose yours are at home hung safely in a wardrobe, ready to be worn when you are next with the king in his palace.'

'You are right,' said Simon, 'they are safely at home . . . in the potting shed. You see, the hat is very useful for carrying the weeds I dig up, and the cape is very comfortable for kneeling on when I'm planting out seedlings. Yes, very comfortable indeed. And no matter, for I am still a musketeer!' added Simon.

Together they continued along the path through the dark, foreboding wood until Roderick asked, 'But Simon, swiftest toothpick this side of Swainsford, as a royal musketeer I am sure you must spend an awful lot of time with the king. You are so lucky. I saw the king once, and that was only the back of his head as he drove past in his carriage.'

'Oh yes, the king,' Simon said grandly. 'The king . . . Well, to be honest with you, I don't really seem to be able to find the time to spend with the king. You know how things are, I always seem so busy, what with the garden to do . . . you know, it won't weed itself. But no matter, for I am still a musketeer.'

Suddenly there was a noise from behind them. Roderick and Simon spun round. 'Wh . . . wh . . . what was that?' Simon asked nervously.

'It sounded like horses galloping this way,' said Roderick drawing his sword and holding it tight in front of him. 'Perhaps it is the enemy about to attack us in this dark, foreboding wood.'

'The enemy, about to attack us in this dark, foreboding wood?' Simon said, looking very anxious and pale.

'Yes, we must prepare,' said Roderick resolutely.

'Prepare to run away?' said Simon.

'No, prepare to fight!'

And almost immediately they seemed to be surrounded by figures who advanced menacingly towards them with swords drawn and evil scowls on their faces. With a brave shout Roderick attacked, whirling his sword this way and that as he fended off the enemy's blows.

With a quiet whimper Simon collapsed to the floor and covered his head with his hands and closed his eyes tight shut.

'Take that and that and that!' called Roderick as his sword clashed time and again with his assailants', and before long he was able to hold his sword up victoriously above his head. 'Look Simon, swiftest toothpick this side of Swainsford, look at them running away. We have beaten them!'

He looked down to see Simon still cowering on the floor and holding his bent and broken toothpick weakly in his hand.

'You know,' said Roderick, 'you told me you were a musketeer, but I fear you are more a musketeer in name than in action.' And with that he strode off, leaving Simon all alone in the dark, foreboding wood.

General theme   Simon had a problem, for although he said he was a musketeer, he did not lead the sort of disciplined life of a musketeer that he needed to. He didn't practise his sword skills, he didn't look after his sword or his musketeer's uniform. It all seemed too much effort, or he felt he had better things to do.

I wonder if we are ever like Simon, when we can't really be bothered to make that bit of effort, to be really disciplined about something?

If we are not disciplined and don't think carefully about exercise, we can easily become unhealthy. The same can be true if we are not careful about what we eat.

And what about other areas in our lives? What about our work or even our relationships with our friends? Do we show real commitment and effort or are we too like Simon?

Christian theme

Simon was certain that he was a musketeer, but when it came down to it, he didn't seem to be bothered to make the effort, and to be really disciplined. In the Bible, Paul says that we need to be like athletes (1 Corinthians 9:25). Athletes have to be very disciplined about what they eat and how much they train or they won't be successful. Some people have felt it very important to show discipline in what they do, every day. Mother Teresa had a strong belief in God, and she knew that, although it might be challenging and sometimes even tiring, she needed to be disciplined about how she led her life to be really able to help and serve others. Her faith made her keen to make the effort day after day.

What motivates us to show commitment and discipline in our own lives?

PSHME ideas

This story can be used to discuss:

- Discipline
- Commitment
- Perseverance
- Values

- Have you ever been part of a sports team where you had to do training? What was the worst thing about the training?
- Do you play a musical instrument? How much do you have to practise?
- If you could pay £100 and be really good at playing your instrument without ever having to practise again, would you pay it?
- Is part of the satisfaction of winning a race knowing that you have trained and worked really hard beforehand?
- Complete the sentence, 'The thing I have worked hardest for is . . .'

Thematic index

Change	Two ugly bugs
Commitment	A good neighbour Simon, swiftest sword this side of Swainsford
Competition	Frank and Ernest
Contentment	The tailor and the apple tree
Courtesy	Frank and Ernest
Determination	Two ugly bugs
Discipline	Simon, swiftest sword this side of Swainsford
Envy	The tailor and the apple tree
Expectations	The new king
Facing challenges	The king's new gift Two ugly bugs
Forgiveness	Farmer Joe
Friendship	A good neighbour
Generosity	The two brothers
Greed	The rich man's gift
Jealousy	The tailor and the apple tree
Judging others	A good neighbour
Making an impression	The king who had no time to be king
New beginnings	The king's new gift

Openness	Farmer Joe
Perceptions	The good neighbour
	The new king
Perseverance	The king's new gift
	Simon, swiftest sword this side of Swainsford
	Two ugly bugs
Possessions	The two brothers
	The tailor and the apple tree
Power	The new king
Priorities	The rich man's gift
Relationships	The king who had no time to be king
Responsibility	Cedric and the beautiful garden
Self-esteem	The king who had no time to be king
Selfishness	The rich man's gift
	The two brothers
Self-sacrifice	The rich man's gift
Sharing	The two brothers
Stereotypes	The new king
Talents	The king who had no time to be king
The environment	Cedric and the beautiful garden
Trust	Cedric and the beautiful garden
Values	Simon, swiftest sword this side of Swainsford
Valuing others	Frank and Ernest

By the same authors

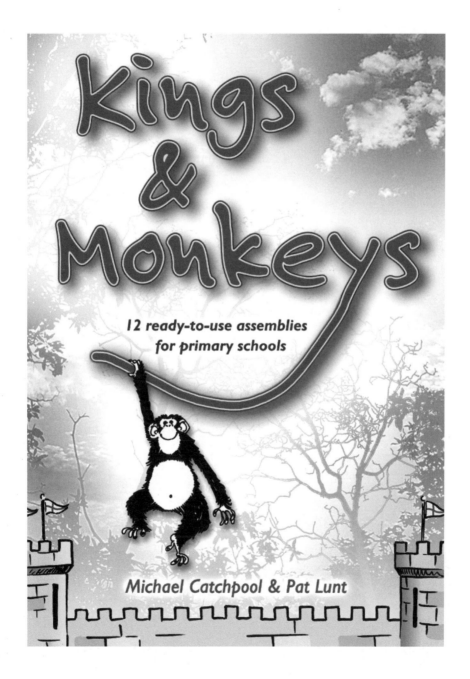

ISBN 1 84003 742 3
Catalogue number 1500429